Altar
Versus
Altars

Deliverance By Sacrifice

Bishop (Dr.) Abraham Chigbundu

ALTAR VERSUS ALTARS
Deliverance by Sacrifice
Copyright 2007
First Edition February 2007
(With Deliverance Prayer Points)

ISBN: 978-38486-1-5

All enquiries & trade orders to:
FREEDOM PUBLICATIONS
VOICE OF FREEDOM MINISTRIES INT'L INC.
21, ADESUWA GRAMMAR SCHOOL ROAD, G.R.A.
P.O. BOX 7240, BENIN CITY. NIGERIA
TEL/FAX 234(0)52-254413
234(0)8022908737
234(0)8023381077
Website: www.voiceoffreedomonline.org
Email: chigbundu@hotmail.com
info@voiceoffreedomonline.org
purchase@voiceoffreedomonline.org

Design + Print
asbot *Graphics*
22, Adifashe Street, opp. MTN Mast, Ladi-Lark, Bariga Lagos
01-8157715, 7933274, 08033671112. E-mail: asbotgraphics@yahoo.com

DEDICATION

This book is dedicated to God The Father, Son, and Holy Spirit for preserving me in all my ministerial assignments and for confirming His words with signs and wonders.

Also to my amiable and lovely Wife, Rev (Mrs) Florence Chigbundu for her constant encouragement, understanding and commitment in the home front as well as in the ministry.

CONTENTS

ACKNOWLEDGEMENTS

My special thanks and gratitude goes to God - The Father, Son, and Holy Spirit for granting me the wisdom and grace as well as the inspiration to write this book.

I am also very grateful to my lovely and understanding wife for always been there for me and also for taking care of our home and the ministry during my ministerial engagements. You are indeed a Priceless Jewel.

Also worthy of mention are my four boys, Emmanuel, Faith, Mike and David You all contributed greatly to the success of this work.

I must not forget the selfless contributions of the

following persons: Pastor Moses Onodua, Pastor Lucky Ehizokhale and Deacon C.C. Isaiah.

I also wish to express my appreciations to Glory Micah for the typesetting and the following persons, Mrs. Smart Nwokoro and Apostle E.C. Lawrence for editing and proofreading this book.

May God richly reward all of you in Jesus' name. Amen.

INTRODUCTION

I have been ministering deliverance to countless number of people for the past twenty-six years with outstanding results. I have engaged in individual, group and mass deliverance sessions lasting for hours with amazing testimonies coming out of them. God has always shown Himself mighty with evidence of His presence everywhere I have had opportunity to minister; I have no regrets whatsoever for being called into this result oriented ministry. I count it a great privilege.

I have written six books on deliverance and many articles, and some of the books are best sellers and are being used in many Bible Colleges as text books in Nigeria, the United States, United Kingdom as well as other parts of the world.

However, one thing has bothered my mind all these years, which is: Why is it that many people's situation refused to change even after they get delivered? I have seen demons leave many lives, with the root cause(s) of their problems identified and rooted out, yet their situations did not change.

I have had cause to minister again and again to make sure that no point of contact or deposit is left anywhere, yet that did not produce any result. I have fasted for some cases for manifestation of evidence, yet in some of these instances, I did not get results. Why? Why? Why?

> *Deliverance does not give you what you want, but rather it opens the gate to what you want.*

This was my question for many years, but thank God for His faithfulness. About a year ago, He spoke to me concerning this and gave me answers to my many questions. Hence, this book *Deliverance by Sacrifice.*

This is the reason for writing this book. The answer is that Deliverance does not give you what you want, but rather it opens the gate to what you want. Deliverance deals with the issues of past events and activities that have created the present problems. Deliverance detaches you from the past, but does not take you to the future. Deliverance ministration destroys the old altars and their voices against us, but does not raise a new altar for the next level.

This is the reason why many people have gone for deliverance ministrations, fasted, gone for all-night meetings and yet the evidence is yet to be seen.

Beyond deliverance is an attempt to give answer and insight to too many questions in the minds of people.

When we destroy the old altar through deliverance ministration, it becomes mandatory for us to raise a new altar with sacrifices for us to move to the next level or provoke evidence. *Welcome to Amazing Insight!*

> *Deliverance detaches you from the past, but does not take you to the future.*

CHAPTER 1

ALTAR
VERSUS
ALTARS

*An **Altar** is a raised or designated*
place where sacrifices are
made to deities.
It is a place where humanity
meets with divinity.

ALTAR
VERSUS
ALTARS

An *Altar* is a raised or designated place where sacrifices are made to deities.

It is a place where humanity meets with divinity.

Biblical altars were generally structures of earth **(Ex. 20:24)** or of hewn stones **(Ex. 20:25)** on which sacrifices were offered. They were generally erected in conspicuous places **(Gen. 22:9)**.

The first altar specifically mentioned in the Bible was the one erected by Noah **(Gen. 8:20)**, although we assume that Adam and the pre-flood patriarchs also used altars for their sacrifices. The first blood sacrifices were mentioned in connection with Adam and Eve (God shedding animal blood to make covering

for them) and their son Abel's offering **(Gen. 3:21, 4:3-4).** Altars were also erected by the patriarch Abraham **(Gen. 12:7, 13:4, 22:9);** by his son Isaac **(Gen. 26:25)** and by Jacob **(Gen. 33:20, 35:1,3)** as well as Moses **(Ex. 17:15** Jehovah Nissi).

It is thus a place of worship. It is a place where humanity enters into covenant with divinity. An altar is a place where sacrifices to deities are made.

Sacrifice is an offering of an animal, something precious or of great value to a deity or deities for propitiation, protection, intervention, vindication, appeasement, covenant, solution, etc.

An altar however, has no power until sacrifice is made on it. Therefore, sacrifice is the power and the voice of an altar.

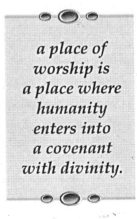

a place of worship is a place where humanity enters into a covenant with divinity.

Sacrifice connotes something of great value. It involves the shedding of blood or killing of something because whatever is brought to the altar for sacrifice *must die.*

Altar versus altars is a spiritual war between two

altars: God's altar and demonic altars against our lives and destinies. It is thus a war between the negative voices speaking against us from the family altars and God's voice from God's altar.

Right from the Old Testament, altar has been a place of shedding of blood. In **Lev. 17:11,** the Bible declares that blood is life and life is blood. It means that blood has voice, and if blood has voice and it is life (which, of course, does not die) then it means that blood speaks. The blood is to speak for atonement for our souls.

> Gen. 4:10 *"...the voice of thy brother's blood crieth unto Me from the ground."*

When Abel was murdered, his blood spoke to God. It was the voice of his blood that God heard.

Blood has voice and speaks. It therefore means that altars have voice through the blood from the sacrifices. Sacrifices therefore become the medium of communication between humanity and divinity at the altar.

An altar has no power until sacrifice is made on it. Therefore, sacrifice is the power and the voice of an altar.

Again, sacrifices attract the presence of the spirits they are offered to.

> **I Cor. 10:20** *"...that the thing which the gentiles sacrifice, they sacrifice to devils, and not to God: and I would not that ye should have fellowship with devils."*

Now, if what the ungodly sacrifice to their gods is to devils, it therefore means that their sacrifices attract the presence of demonic powers and the blood of their sacrifices will speak in favour of those who made the sacrifice or on behalf of those it was made for.

Sacrifice attracts the presence of spirits.

> *And Noah builded an altar unto the LORD; and took of every clean beast, and of every clean fowl, and offered burnt offerings on the altar. And the Lord smelled a sweet savour; and the Lord said in His heart, I will not again curse the ground any more for man's sake; for the imagination of man's heart is evil from his youth; neither will I again smite any more everything living, as I have done. While the earth remaineth, seedtime and harvest, and cold and heat, and summer and winter, and day and night shall not cease.* **(Gen. 8:20-22)**

Also, **Gen. 9:1-19** states the various promises and

covenants God made with Noah when He came to attend to the sacrifice of Noah. When the sacrifice attracts the presence of the spirits it is offered to, the next thing that follows is pronouncements and covenants.

> *Blood has voice and speaks. It therefore means that altars have voice through the blood from the sacrifices.*

In **Gen. 15:1-19**, God demanded sacrifice from Abram so that He could enter into covenant with him. In **vs. 12-18,** the scriptures states thus:

> *"And when the sun was going down, a deep sleep fell upon Abram; and lo, an horror of great darkness fell upon him. And He said unto Abram, Know of a surety that thy seed shall be a stranger in a land that is not theirs, and shall serve them; and they shall afflict them 400 years; and also that nation, whom they shall serve, will I judge: and afterward shall they come out with great substance. And thou shalt go to thy fathers in peace; thou shalt be buried in a good old age. But in the fourth generation they shall come hither again; for the iniquity of the Amorites is not yet full. And it came to pass, that, when the sun went down, and it was dark, behold a smoking furnace, and a burning lamp that passed between those*

> *pieces. In the same day the Lord made a covenant with Abram, saying, 'Unto thy seed have I given this land, from the river of Egypt unto the great river, the river Euphrates."*

In the above portion, God told Abram about his seed and what will happen to them hundreds of years from then even when the patriarch Abram had no child.

In **Gen. 22:15-17,** God's presence was attracted by Abraham's sacrifice of his only son, Isaac.

> *"And the angel of the Lord called unto Abraham out of heaven the second time, and said, By Myself have I sworn, saith the Lord, for because thou hast done this thing, and hast not withheld thy son, thine only son: that in blessing I will bless thee, and multiplying I will multiply thy seed as the stars of the heaven, and as the sand which is upon the seashore; and thy seed shall possess the gate of his enemies."*

By these words, God blessed Abraham and entered into a generational covenant of blessing with him because of the sacrifice.

In **Judges 6:25-26, 34,** the Bible reports that:

> *"And it came to pass the same night that the Lord said unto him, Take thy father's young*

> *bullock, even the second bullock of seven*
> *years old, and throw down the altar of Baal*
> *that thy father hath, and cut down the grove*
> *that is by it: And build an altar unto the*
> *Lord thy God upon the top of this rock, in*
> *the ordered place, and take the second*
> *bullock, and offer a burnt sacrifice with the*
> *wood of the grove which thou shalt cut*
> *down...But the Spirit of the Lord came upon*
> *Gideon, and he blew a trumpet; and Abiezer*
> *was gathered after him."*

Here, it was Gideon's sacrifice on the new altar that attracted the Spirit of God on him and consequently gave victory over the Midianites and his subsequent elevation to the office of a Judge in Israel. This became possible even though he was the least in a poor family in the tribe of Manasseh.

2 Chron. 1:6-12 also gives more credence to this issue:

> *"And Solomon went up thither to the*
> *brazen altar before the Lord, which was at*
> *the tabernacle of the congregation, and*
> *offered a thousand burnt offerings upon it.*
> *In that night did God appear unto Solomon,*
> *and said unto him, Ask what I shall give*
> *thee. And Solomon said unto God, Thou*
> *hast shewed great mercy unto David my*
> *father, and hast made me to reign in his*

stead. Now, O Lord God, let Thy promise unto David my father be established: for Thou hast made me king over a people like the dust of the earth in multitude. Give me now wisdom and knowledge, that I may go out and come in before this people: for who can judge this Thy people, that is so great? And God said to Solomon, because this was in thine heart, and thou hast not asked riches, wealth, or honour, nor the life of thine enemies, neither yet hast asked long life; but hast asked wisdom and knowledge for thyself, that thou mayest judge My people, over whom I have made thee king: wisdom and knowledge is granted unto thee; and I will give thee riches, and wealth, and honour, such as none of the kings have had that have been before thee, neither shall there any after thee have the like."

Here, Solomon's one thousand burnt offerings on the altar attracted God's presence and He spoke to him to ask what he needed. God's presence will always be attracted whenever our sacrifice comes on His altar.

> *God's presence will always be attracted whenever our sacrifice comes on His altar.*

In the same way, Satan's presence will always be attracted whenever sacrifice comes on his altar.

Satan is a specialist in counterfeiting anything that God does. He saw that great and generational covenants are entered into through blood by God, so he counterfeited it and used it to bring humanity into bondage.

CHAPTER

SINS
OF OUR
FATHERS

*Our fathers have sinned, and are not; and
we have borne their iniquities. Servants
have ruled over us: there is none that doth
deliver us out of their hand.*

TWO

THE SINS
OF OUR
FATHERS

"Our fathers have sinned, and are not; and we have borne their iniquities. Servants have ruled over us: there is none that doth deliver us out of their hand. We gat our bread with the peril of our lives because of the sword of the wilderness. Our skin was black like an oven because of the terrible famine. They ravished the women in Zion, and the maids in the cities of Judah. Princes are hanged up by their hand: the faces of elders were not honoured. They took the young men to grind, and the children fell under the wood. The elders have ceased from the gate, the young men from their musick. The joy of our heart is ceased; our dance is turned into mourning. The crown is fallen from our head: woe unto us, that we have sinned! For this our heart is faint; for these things our eyes are dim."   **(Lam. 5:7-17)**

'Our fathers have sinned and are not!' They are dead. We may not have seen or known some of our fathers, yet their actions or sins in the past seem to have strange consequences on us.

The above passage states the numerous consequences of our fathers' sins, which include:

(a)   As a result of their sins, servants now rule over us.

Those who ought to be serving us are now our masters. In **Gen. 1:28**, the Bible says,

> *"And God blessed them, and said...Be fruitful and multiply, and replenish the earth, and subdue it; and have dominion over the fish of the sea, over the fowl of the air, and over everything that moveth upon the earth."*

From this portion, it is clear that God's intention for man at creation was that he should have dominion over everything He has created. But what do we see today? The contrary is the case, where what we were commanded to rule over is now ruling over us. This is a clear sign of bondage

> *God's intention for man... was that he should have dominion over everything ...But today, contrary is the case.*

and it is contrary to God's ordained will for us.

Today, sickness, poverty, non-achievement, disgrace and shame have become our masters. Why? Our fathers sinned.

(b)   We seek for deliverance in many areas of our lives, yet it seems our deliverance prayers and ministrations are not yielding the desired result.

Why? Our fathers have sinned.

(c)   We get our daily bread with much struggle.

We make so much effort with little or no result at all. It seems 'all' our efforts can produce is just to feed our stomach. But the question is, 'Is that all we were created to achieve?' In many cases today, all that many succeed to achieve is just to feed themselves and families, whereas others build factories and other great edifices and business empires.

(d)   Our skins have turned black because of much hardship

(e)   Our women and our young girls have been sexually violated.

They have been forced by circumstances beyond

their control into sex markets. The slogan on most lips today is, 'use what you have to get what you need.' Our women's lives are thus being cut short; many are widows; others are orphans, while yet a multitude of others have died without fulfilling the purpose for which they were created

> *We make so much effort with little or no result at all. It seems 'all' our efforts can produce is just to feed our stomach*

because of HIV/AIDS which they contacted through the sin of immorality.

Our young girls in the villages, secondary schools and tertiary institutions are turned into prostitutes; many of them against their consciences' good judgment and upbringing. They do not understand why they are doing the ignorable trade our fathers sinned.

(f)   Our princes hands are tied.

Our noble youths with great talents and potential are roaming the streets. They have been repackaged; their destinies have been tampered with hence they now resort to armed robbery, fraud, drug peddling and all manner of evil vices just to make it in life. Why? The sins of our fathers have affected their potentials.

(g)   Our elders are no longer honoured.

Our society has been turned upside down. The young now rule over the elderly because of ill-gotten wealth. Men of questionable characters are now traditional rulers; young men with money and power have bagged different chieftaincy titles. Grey hair is no longer a mark of old age, rather the evidence of poverty and a fruitless life. What exactly is wrong with us?

(h)   Our youths have become slaves in various nations of the world even with their degrees.

They grind in many prisons and ghettos of the world. Why? They are searching for answers to the many questions confronting and bugging their minds and lives. They are looking for solutions from anywhere they can find it. Why is it so? Who is to blame? Our fathers have sinned.

(i)   Our children have become slaves in their fathers' houses.

They have joined the army in their teens and are killed without mercy. They have been sold into slavery and roam the streets selling all manner of wears while their contemporaries are in schools pursuing better future.

(J)   Our elders are no longer at the city gates to deliberate the affairs of their cities.

They have left their place in pursuit of wealth. There is no more integrity and honesty in our land because the elders, who are supposed to teach and impart knowledge, discipline and core family values to the younger ones, are now wallowing deeply in corruptions. No one is considering posterity in their actions. Our family, village and city gates are without elders. Our valuable cultures and traditions, as well as family and village values are no more observed. Why? Our fathers have sinned.

> *They have left their place in pursuit of wealth. There is no more integrity and honesty in our land because the elders, who are supposed to teach and impart knowledge, ... are now wallowing deeply in corruptions.*

(k)   Our joy is gone.

We have lost the sweetness of life. Tears are constantly in our eyes because our seeds die in the ground and harvest has continuously eluded us. What did we do wrong? Why are we suffering like this?

(l)   Our dance has turned into mourning.

Where we expected joy, we saw sorrows. When we expected success, behold it was failure that greeted us. When we expected fruitfulness, we saw barrenness. We wake up with sorrows and sleep with tears, only to go through the same routine all over again the next day: beginning with struggle and ending with yet more struggles. Why? Where is our God? Has He forsaken us? No, our fathers have sinned.

(m)   Our crown has fallen from our head

What a tragedy! The honour and glory of our lives have been taken away from us.

(n)   Our heart faints.

We are confused about life. We no longer know which way to turn to; we are fed up and tired because we seem to be repeating history and the negative one at that. Yes, our heart faints because our efforts produce nothing but tears and sorrows. Why? Our fathers have sinned.

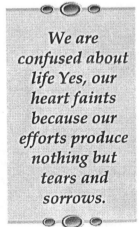

We are confused about life Yes, our heart faints because our efforts produce nothing but tears and sorrows.

(o) Our eyes are dim.

Our eyes cannot see afar off. We seem not to have insight or foresight into issues of life any more.

What is happening to us? Our fathers have sinned and are not, yet we bear the consequences of their sins.

CHAPTER 3

FAMILY
PATTERNS

*Satan knows the mystery behind the blood on the
altar hence he manipulated our fathers to build
altars and sacrifice on them to enable him and
his demonic powers to lay hold on members of
the family and continue their wicked activities.*

THREE

FAMILY PATTERNS

O ur fathers erected strange altars in pursuit of their comfort and that of future generations without considering the consequences of such altars.

They served strange gods and sacrificed to idols, Satan's representatives. Their sacrifices on such devilish altars have become voices that challenge us at the point of success.

These altars were the places of worship and where covenants were made and sealed with the blood from the sacrifices. The

> *Our fathers erected strange altars in pursuit of their comfort and that of future generations without considering the consequences of such altars.*

altars thus became the basis for family patterns and history; and because the devil cannot fight any man outside his family pattern and history, there is usually a repetition of family negative history which finds expression through the family altars.

Family altars have voices and they speak. Satan knows the mystery behind the blood on the altar hence he manipulated our fathers to build altars and sacrifice on them to enable him and his demonic powers to lay hold on members of the family and continue their wicked activities.

A lot of the troubles we face in life did not start with us; they are continuation of what had been in existence before us. They continue because we have not given them the attention they require. They continue because some of us believe that what our fathers did will have no effect on us. Oh, how wrong we are, and how we have allowed ourselves to be deceived! The Bible has made it clear that through one man, sin entered into the world and through one man

> *A lot of the troubles we face in life did not start with us; they are continuation of what had been in existence before us.*

(Jesus), righteousness also comes.

Was it not Abraham's act of faith that has made us all partakers and heirs of his blessings? Is there anyone alive today who knew Abraham physically? **Heb. 3:4** says that *"Every house is builded by some man."*

Child of God, this plague ravaging the family was provoked by somebody in the past. I want you to know that there is no new spirit fighting you. No. It is the same spirit that fought your parents to the point they are now or were in the past. It is the same power that is denying you access to the next level of your life.

The family altars have set the limit of the progress of family members, and whoever gets to that limit will have to be stopped. The altars, however, will not speak until you get to the limit or boundary of their target. They are set to operate with time and season and so until you get there, they will not speak. Please, do not ignore this information simply because you do not see its importance

> *Was it not Abraham's act of faith that has made us all partakers and heirs of his blessings?*

now; it is only because the time for its manifestation has not yet come.

The easiest way to understand the evil manifestations of these strange altars is to take a close look at the happenings in your life and those of members of your family on both sides of your parents. A closer and careful study will enhance your knowledge on this matter.

BIBLICAL EXAMPLE

Abraham's Family

Abraham was called out of his heathen family by God. He did not ask God to call him; it was God's choice. He saw his background, yet He called him. Abraham was 75 years old and his wife Sarah was 65 years when God called him. He had already married and his wife was barren before God called him. It took another 25 years before his wife could give birth to a child. If there was anybody who should not have problems in life, it should be father Abraham and his family because God called him. But the contrary was the case.

A close examination of the following will give you a clearer picture of this matter:

(a)   Barrenness In Family

Sarah, Abraham's wife, was barren
Rebecca, Isaac's wife, was also barren
Her daughter in-law, Rachael, Jacob's beloved wife, was barren as well

(b)   Limited No. Of Children

1.   Abraham had only Isaac with his wife Sarah
2.   Isaac had only Esau and Jacob with Rebecca
3.   Jacob had only Joseph and Benjamin with Rachael
4.   Joseph had only Manasseh and Ephraim

(c)   Loss Of First Son's Birthright

1.   Ishmael was the first biological son of Abraham, but lost the birthright to Isaac
2.   Esau was the first son of Isaac but lost his birthright to Jacob
3.   Reuben, been the first son of Jacob, lost his birthright to Joseph
4.   Manasseh also was the first son of Joseph, but lost his birthright to his younger brother, Ephraim

What do you say about a family of six: four males and two females, with each of the males going blind at the age of twenty-five? Strange altars spoke against each of them at that age. Someone must stop these strange voices against the male folks of this family.

In the course of ministering to people, I have come across different families with similar occurrences e.g. some of the families experience divorce amongst their female folks at certain ages. Others experience divorce as soon as they give birth to male or female children. While yet for others, the male folks have stable marriages but live in abject poverty and their females hardly ever get married even though they enjoy relative affluence.

I once met a family that hardly gave birth to male children. They could have up to eight female children without a single male.

A beloved brother of 48 years met me sometime ago for ministration because his sisters usually died at the age of 29+; they did not get to become 30 years. On investigation, I discovered that his ancestors had buried a king with a living young woman of about 30 years and the lady had sworn as she was being buried alive that the daughters of her killers would never live beyond her age. That incident had happened about 100 years before this brother or any of his sisters was born.

In all of the above examples, the people who experienced the mysterious happenings were not the generation that raised the altars and yet the voices of those altars still affected them.

I have seen families where anybody with a bright future dies prematurely and sometimes, in mysterious circumstances.

In some families, you will see uncompleted buildings that have been standing for years. Why? Those who started them wanted to break the limitation of the evil one in the family without destroying these altars and their voices and so they were stopped by the altars.

Those strange altars are the basis for evil patterns in our families. When you look around, you will see the evil patterns occurring either from your mother's or father's lineage.

Have you ever wondered why your father struggled so much like his own father and you have now taken the same position of suffering. Though you blame it on the economy and your inability to go to the university, the truth is that the level you want to get to in life has never been attained by anybody, dead or alive in your family. Something stopped them and what was it? The altar. Have you thought about it?

The altars and their wicked voices have set boundaries and limitation in the family and as long as there is no new altar to stop their voices, they will keep on speaking until somebody stops them.

> *...And as long as there is no new altar to stop their voices, they will keep on speaking until somebody stops them.*

EXAMPLES OF EVIL PATTERNS IN THE FAMILY

Poverty, divorce at certain age, untimely death, certain sickness, barrenness, late marriages, non-achievements, backwardness, poverty at old age, mental problems, etc.

When you check the occurrences of the above in the family you come from, you will understand the mystery of the altars our fathers raised. These altars have stopped us where they stopped our fathers. Time does not solve spiritual problems; rather it complicates spiritual problems because in some cases, nobody is alive to give us the details of what happened. This is why God gave us the Holy Ghost who knows all things to help us.

Many people are repeating their family history or patterns and do not know because the patterns have turned digital. Our fathers experienced the analogue manifestation in their time, but ours has gone scientific.

Why did your father stop where he stopped? Why did your mother stop where she did? What about your uncles and aunties why did they stop where they did? And why are you and your siblings going through the same experiences? Why are the male folks in your family, village and tribe going through this kind of tragedy? Think and do something now! If it was started by somebody, then somebody can stop it and that person is *you.*

What is fighting you is the family spirit which you have ignored. *The lion you refuse to kill will kill you.* The issues you refuse to confront will confront you.

The enemy of your destiny will want you to ignore him and believe that he is not responsible for your pains and sorrow so that he can finish you, but God forbid that you will continue in ignorance! *Ignorance is the strength of the oppressor.* This book will destroy ignorance in you and empower you with knowledge.

You cannot confront what you have not identified. What you know determines your impact in life. What you know makes you valuable to your generation. What you know determines your size in life. It is the truth you know that guarantees your freedom because you cannot perform beyond your level of knowledge. Knowledge eliminates mysteries out of issues of life. Knowledge ends needless sufferings and pains.

> *It is the truth you know that guarantees your freedom because you cannot perform beyond your level of knowledge.*

CHAPTER 4

GIDEON
AND HIS
FATHER'S ALTAR

*And the children of Israel did evil in the sight
of the Lord: and the Lord delivered them into
the hand of Midian seven years. And the
hand of Midian prevailed against Israel*

FOUR

4

GIDEON AND HIS FATHER'S ALTAR

And the children of Israel did evil in the sight of the Lord: and the Lord delivered them into the hand of Midian seven years. And the hand of Midian prevailed against Israel: and because of the Midianites the children of Israel made them the dens which are in the mountains, and caves, and strongholds. And so it was, when Israel had sown, that the Midianites came up, and the Amalekites, and the children of the east, even they came up against them; and they encamped against them, and destroyed the increase of the earth, till thou come unto Gaza, and left no sustenance for Israel, neither sheep, nor ox, nor ass. For they came up with their cattle and their tents, and they came as grasshoppers for multitude; for both they

*and their camels were without number:
and they entered into the land to destroy
it. And Israel was greatly impoverished
because of the Midianites; and the
children of Israel cried unto the Lord. And
it came to pass, when the children of Israel
cried unto the Lord because of the
Midianites, that the Lord sent a prophet
unto the children of Israel, which said
unto them, Thus saith the Lord God of
Israel, I brought you up from Egypt, and
brought you forth out of the house of
bondage.* **(Judges 6:1-8)**

*And there came an angel of the Lord, and
sat under an oak which was in Ophrah,
that pertained unto Joash the Abiezrite:
and his son Gideon threshed wheat by the
winepress, to hide it from the Midianites.
And the angel of the Lord appeared unto
him, and said into him, The Lord is with
thee, thou mighty man of valour. And
Gideon said unto him, Oh my Lord, if the
Lord be with us, why then is all this
befallen us? And where be all His
miracles which our fathers told us of,
saying, Did not the Lord bring us up from
Egypt? But now the Lord hath forsaken
us, and delivered us into the hands of the
Midianites. And the Lord looked upon
him, and said, Go in this thy might, and*

*thou shalt save Israel from the hand of
the Midianites: have not I sent thee? And
he said unto him, Oh my Lord,
wherewith shall I save Israel? Behold,
my family is poor in Manasseh, and I am
the least in my father's house. And the
Lord said unto him, Surely I will be with
thee, and thou shalt smite the Midianites
as one man.*   (Judges 6:11-16)

<u>Vs. 25-35</u>
*And it came to pass the same night, that
the Lord said unto him, Take thy father's
young bullock, even the second bullock of
seven years old, and throw down the altar
of Baal that thy father hath, and cut down
the grove that is by it: and build an altar
unto the Lord thy God upon the top of this
rock, in the ordered place, and take the
second bullock, and offer a burnt sacrifice
with the wood of the grove which thou
shalt cut down. Then Gideon took ten
men of his servants, and did as the Lord
had said unto him: and so it was, because
he feared his father's household, and the
men of the city, that he could not do it by
day, that he did it by night. And when the
men of the city arose early in the morning,
behold, the altar of Baal was cast down,
and the grove was cut down that was by
it, and the second bullock was offered*

upon the altar that was built. And they said one to another, Who hath done this thing? And when they inquired and asked, they said, Gideon the son of Joash hath done this thing. Then the men of the city said unto Joash, Bring out thy son, that he may die: because he hath cast down the altar of Baal, and because he hath cut down the grove that was by it. And Joash said unto all that stood against him, Will ye plead for Baal? Will ye save him? He that will plead for him, let him be put to death whilst it is yet morning: if he be a god, let him plead for himself, because one hath cast down his altar. Therefore on that day he called him Jerub-baal, saying, Let Baal plead against him, because he hath thrown down his altar. Then all the Midianites and the Amalekites and the children of the east were gathered together, and went over, and pitched in the valley of Jezreel. But the Spirit of the Lord came upon Gideon, and he blew a trumpet; and Abiezer was gathered after him. And he sent messengers throughout all Manasseh; who also gathered after him: and he sent messengers unto Asher, and unto Zebulun, and unto Naphtali; and they came up to meet them.

Until you discover, you may not recover. Discovery is the key that opens the door of all recoveries. You cannot kill the enemy you do not know. You cannot confront what you have not identified.

Gideon was packaged by heaven to be a judge in Israel, but he arrived in a family that had raised strange altars. He did not choose his birthplace or his parents. God did and He did it for a purpose. This family and the entire nation of Israel had been crying to God for a deliverer. Poverty and suffering have been the order of the day.

Gideon could not change the situation because he did not know what was wrong. And even though he had God's hand on him, he could not become what he was created to become. He joined the toiling in the family; he encountered poverty and became a part of it though he was destined to be rich.

> *Discovery is the key that opens the door of all recoveries. You cannot kill the enemy you do not know. You cannot confront what you have not identified.*

From **vs. 11** he had an encounter that changed his life. When the angel announced to him who he actually was and the assurance of God's hand on his life, he asked the same question that multitudes are asking today: *If God is with me, why am I going through all these? Where is the manifestation of His promises to His children? Has God not forsaken His own?*

The reason why we ask such questions is because there are no evidence accompanying our deliverance, prayers and fasting, confession of the scriptures and quoting of the same. As a result, some of us are confused because of the mockery of our detractors. Our present experiences are contrary to the Bible we read and quote. We ask these questions because answers to our prayers are delayed and prophesies are not fulfilled. Why?

> *Our present experiences are contrary to the Bible we read and quote. We ask these questions because answers to our prayers are delayed and prophesies are not fulfilled.*

Our fathers have sinned and we now suffer for their sins. They used their tradition to render the word of God of no effect in our lives through their strange altars **(Matt. 15:6ᵇ).**

In essence, the Angel announced to Gideon:

> *you have been chosen by God to end the siege*
> *in your family. God has chosen you to end*
> *the poverty in the family. This enemy that*
> *has terrorized generation after generation*
> *will end their occupation in your time.*
> *Gideon, you were created for this purpose.'*

Gideon reminded the Angel that he was the least in a poor family in Manasseh. Child of God, the issue is not **where** you are, but **who** you are. If you can identify who you are, then you can change the situation around you.

In **vs. 25-27**, God instructed him on what to do to end the suffering in his life and family.

> *And it came to pass the same night, that the*
> *Lord said unto him, Take thy father's*
> *young bullock, even the second bullock of*
> *seven years old, and throw down the altar*
> *of Baal that thy father hath, and cut down*
> *the grove that is by it: and build an altar*
> *unto the Lord thy God upon the top of this*
> *rock, in the ordered place, and take the*
> *second bullock, and offer a burnt sacrifice*
> *with the wood of the grove which thou*
> *shalt cut down. Then Gideon took ten men*
> *of his servants, and did as the Lord had*
> *said unto him: and so it was, because he*
> *feared his father's household, and the men*

of the city, that he could not do it by day, that he did it by night.

God showed him what was wrong in the family and the entire nation. He showed him the source of his poverty, suffering, struggling without evidence, labouring without reward: the altar in his father's house. it was not Gideon's altar, but his father's altar which was the altar that connects the entire nation of Israel.

GOD'S INSTRUCTIONS

1.   Destroy the altar of Baal in your father's house
2.   Build another altar for God and use the second cow of seven years old amongst your father's cows and offer it as a **burnt sacrifice** on the **new altar.**

Dear reader, in these two instructions lie the key to your total victory. The first instruction is to *destroy the old altar.* This is where deliverance comes in. Deliverance is dealing with the issues of the past **(altar)** that has stopped us in the same spot where the past generation stopped. Deliverance is cutting the link between the past and the present so that you can move to the next level of your life. It is the removing of the

Egyptian seed that has followed us from Egypt so that we can enter Canaan and enjoy the milk and honey in the land.

> *Deliverance is dealing with the issues of the past (altar) that has stopped us in the same spot where the past generation stopped.*

Deliverance is the starting point of reaching our destiny, but that is not all there is to it. It requires much more than just being placed or positioned at the starting line. God, the Almighty knew that it would take more than just destroying the old altar for Gideon to become what He had created him to be.

The old altar's assignment is to keep us where it kept the past generation. Therefore, when we destroy it, we are ready to move to the level the past generation could not get to or enter.

God said to Gideon, *build a new altar and sacrifice on it.* Why?

Until there is a new **altar and sacrifice,** we will not enter the next level. It is the *voice of the new sacrifice on the new altar that will speak in our favour.*

The old altar was empowered by sacrifice. Sacrifice attracted demonic powers to operate in the family. The new altar and sacrifices disarm these demonic powers and attract God's Spirit, who speaks in our favour.

> *Until there is a new altar and sacrifice, we will not enter the next level. It is the voice of the new sacrifice on the new altar that will speak in our favour.*

God's children often stop at destroying the old altar, which is deliverance, but refuse to follow Gideon's examples. Many people are prepared to go for thirty days deliverance ministration, forty days fasting and prayer, but yet they are not ready to build a new altar and sacrifice on it. They are not ready to pay the price for the next level. This is the reason why there are many deliverance and prayers, yet very little result.

Sacrifice attracts the presence of spirits. Sacrifice on God's altar attracts the spirit of God to intervene in a man's affairs **(Isa. 49:24-26)**.

God is ready to contend with whatsoever contends with your destiny, but you must attract His presence with your sacrifice. If you want your enemies or the attackers of your destiny to eat their flesh and drink their own blood, then you must be ready to attract God's presence with your sacrifice.

The sacrifices of our fathers on their altars armed demonic powers to operate in the family. Therefore, our sacrifice on God's altar will stop such spirits from operating.

> *Sacrifice attracts the presence of spirits. Sacrifice on God's altar attracts the spirit of God to intervene in a man's affairs.*

Gideon's lifting came after he obeyed God fully. The elders of the land came and saw the destruction of the old altar and the sacrifice on the new altar. A new altar and sacrifice must replace the old, for manifestations of our desires to take place after deliverance.

It is the voice of our new altar that will speak us into our destiny. The voice of the new altar will shut up the voice of the old one. The voice of the old altar is the voice of witchcraft that is against our destiny. The voice of the new altar is the voice of the Spirit of God that speaks for our lifting and success in life.

From **vs. 33,** the new altar and sacrifice of Gideon began to speak and the Spirit of the Lord came upon Gideon. The enemy had gathered to destroy the increase of the land as before, but was not aware this time, that a certain young man from a relatively poor family had done something which the past generation was not able to do. They were not aware that the old altar, which was the legal ground for oppressing Israel, had been destroyed. They were not aware that a young man, who was held captive by the old altar, had suddenly changed his position and raised a new altar that would permanently disarm them.

> *The voice of the new altar is the voice of the Spirit of God that speaks for our lifting and success in life*

Gideon blew his trumpet when the Spirit of the Lord came upon him on the new altar and his helpers heard his voice for the first time. They heard a new sound and rushed to Gideon. His helpers came from his village and tribe where his family was known to be poor and where they knew him to be the least in the family. His helpers came from the families of the elders who sought his death before now. And what did they hear? The voice of a man on a new altar!

Do you know why you have remained on one level for many years now? Your helpers could not hear your voice.

There is a new sound for your next level and that is what your helpers for the next level are waiting to hear; but the old altar has denied you this new sound, hence your helpers have not heard your voice.

There are two most important people assigned by God to help you fulfill your destiny. They are your *Helpers* and *Advertisers*. Your Advertisers are to introduce you to your destiny helpers. Just a word from them projects your person and potentials. Your Helpers are rather receiving strange information about you; hence they have become your *'hinderers'* instead of being your helpers. They heard the voice of your detractors inspired by the old altars.

At one point or the other, you may have come across your destiny helpers, but they could not identify you because of the garment of shame and disgrace which the powers of the old altar have put on you.

But hear me. *From now onward, your advertisers will speak in your favour at the right place and to the right people!*

When John the Baptist introduced Jesus in the midst of the crowd, they knew Him for the first time. And God confirmed it by introducing Him to the crowd as His beloved Son **(Matt. 3:13-17)**.

You need somebody to introduce you to your destiny helpers. You need somebody to speak in your favour to the right people. Gideon's helpers were thirty-two thousand men who had just gathered unto a non-entity of yesterday. They were ready to take instructions from him. This was how Gideon became Israel's judge and leader who delivered them from the hand of the Midianites. Gideon went from being a *'nobody'* to *'somebody'*- from *the least* to the *most important,* from *poor family* to the *richest family* in Manasseh.

You can change the evil occurrence in your family. You can become what God created you to become. You can become the Gideon of your family. You can become the answer and solution your family has been waiting and crying for over the years. Do you know you were born again

You can become the Gideon of your family. You can become the answer and solution your family has been waiting and crying for over the years.

for this purpose? Do you know you were chosen by God even before you were born to bring the deliverance your family and generation has been waiting for?

Do not disappoint them. Do something to end the siege in your family. Do something to end the poverty and non-achievement in your family. Pay the price and take the delivery. Build a new altar and sacrifice on it for a change to take place. For a change to take place, it will cost you something valuable. Child of God, take note that the enemy of your destiny does not want you to make the right sacrifice because your fathers' sacrifices empowered them in the first place; and if you build a new altar for God and sacrifice on it, they know that their power over your life will be broken forever.

> *Pay the price and take the delivery. Build a new altar and sacrifice on it for a change to take place.*

Defy their voices and do it! Change your position like Gideon. Take your name out from that ancestral list. Cut off your link from the family circle of negative events. Do what your parents could not do and achieve what they could not achieve

.Gideon became Israel's judge without campaigning or lobbying any tribe. He paid the price and took the delivery of his destiny.

God showed him how to achieve much with little. Instead of using the thirty-two thousand soldiers who had responded to his call, God told him to use three hundred to defeat the three nations which had come to destroy them.

When you destroy the old altar and build a new one with valuable sacrifice, the following happen:

- The first thing that will take place is the coming of the Spirit of God on you - a new anointing for great achievement and greatness.

- Second, your helpers and advertisers will hear your voice and respond to you.

- The grace to accomplish much with little will come on you

- You will defeat your enemies no matter how many they are

- You will step into the next level of your life which is the manifestation of your destiny

- You will begin to rule what once ruled you

- You will change your status and that of your family

- You will end poverty in your life and family

- Your will be in charge of the affairs of your life

CHAPTER 5

THE POWER
OF
SACRIFICE

*When God was ready to solve the sin problem
once and for all, He chose the way of
sacrifice...He did this to show us the way out
of stubborn situations. He offered His only
begotten Son on the cross for our redemption.*

THE POWER OF SACRIFICE

FIVE

5

Sacrifice is the offering of animals or something valuable on the altar to deities. This could be for reasons such as propitiation, success, healing, progress, good marriage, stoppage of evil occurrences, etc.

Sacrifice, which involves shedding of blood, becomes the power of the altar. Altars are empowered by the blood from sacrifices.

Because of the voice of the blood on the altar, many people are going through some mysterious situations in their lives. The voice from the strange altars of our fathers has kept on speaking because we have not brought a new sacrifice to stop their voice.

When God was ready to solve the sin problem once and for all, He chose the way of sacrifice. He could have spoken from His throne and everything would have worked according to His command. He did this to show us the way out of stubborn situations. He offered His only begotten Son on the cross for our redemption.

> *"Jesus, when He had cried again with a loud voice, yielded up the ghost. And, behold, the veil of the temple was rent in twain from the top to the bottom; and the earth did quake, and the rocks rent; and the graves were opened; and many bodies of the saints which slept arose, and came out of the graves after His resurrection, and went into the holy city, and appeared unto many."*
> (Matt. 27:50-53)

Today, that supreme sacrifice produced the blood of Jesus which has spoken billions into the kingdom of God. That blood is still speaking over two thousand years ago. It spoke yesterday; it is speaking right now and will speak after now. That blood does not loose its power. It reaches to the highest

The blood of Jesus is still speaking. It spoke yesterday; it is speaking right now and will speak after now. That blood does not loose its power.

mountain and it flows to the lowest valley.When the blood of Jesus touched the earth from he cross, the earth shook, graves were opened and men and women held captives against their wills resurrected. They were released from the old altar and came out with Jesus on the resurrection morning and walked in the streets of Jerusalem.

These were men and women who had been forgotten and written off, yet they were seen by those who had drawn conclusions about them. What happened? The new altar and the blood of the Lamb of God spoke freedom to them and they were released.

I prophesy to you that whatever has held you bound against your will shall hear a new voice and release you by force in Jesus' name!

Everywhere they have written you off, despised or shut doors against you, the same people shall desire to see you again. You will shine again. In places where you were disgraced and humiliated, by the voice of the new altar, you shall be celebrated!

"Behold, at that time I will undo all that afflict thee: and I will save her that halteth, and gather her that was driven out; and I will get them praise and fame in every land

where they have been put to shame. At that time will I bring you again, even in the time that I gather you: for I will make you a name and a praise among all people of the earth, when I turn back your captivity before your eyes, saith the Lord."   (Zeph. 3:19-20)

This scripture will be fulfilled in your life in Jesus' name. Amen.

"And Noah builded an altar unto the Lord; and took of every clean beast, and of every clean fowl, and offered burnt offerings on the altar. And the Lord smelled a sweet savour; and the Lord said in his heart, I will not again curse the ground any more for man's sake; for the imagination of man's heart is evil from his youth; neither will I again smite any more everything living, as I have done. While the earth remaineth, seedtime and harvest, and cold and heat, and summer and winter, and day and night shall not cease."   (Gen. 8:20-22)

NOAH'S EXPERIENCE

When Noah and his children came out of the ark, he raised an altar and offered a sacrifice to the Lord which attracted God's attention. Consequently, God entered into a covenant with

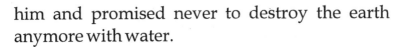
him and promised never to destroy the earth anymore with water.

ABRAHAM'S CASE GEN. 15:1-2

Abraham complained to God about his childlessness situation and God responded by demanding a sacrifice from him. When he offered the sacrifice, God entered into a covenant with him that day and told him the future of his children.

> *"In the same day the Lord made a covenant with Abram, saying, Unto thy seed have I given this land, from the river of Egypt unto the great river, the river Euphrates..."*
> **(Gen. 15:18)**

Whenever a sacrifice comes on God's altar, it attracts His presence and when He comes, He speaks.

Gen. 22:15-18

When Abraham offered his only son, Isaac on Mount Moriah, God swore by Himself to bless Abraham and multiply his seed. He thus entered into an everlasting covenant of blessing with Abraham and his seed, and today, we are all beneficiaries of that covenant of blessings.

SOLOMON'S CASE (2 CHRON. 1:6-12)

When God saw 1,000 sacrifices of Solomon, He appeared to him in the night and asked him what he wanted.

Sacrifice attracts the presence of God to intervene in human affairs that have baffled us.

> *"Shall the prey be taken from the mighty, or the lawful captive delivered? But thus saith the Lord, Even the captives of the mighty shall be take away, and the prey of the terrible shall be delivered: for I will contend with him that contendeth with thee, and I will save thy children. And I will feed them that oppress thee with their own flesh; and they shall be drunken with their own blood, as with sweet wine: and all flesh shall know that I the Lord am thy Saviour and thy Redeemer the mighty One of Jacob."* **(Isa. 49:24-26)**

This is only possible when God comes down to intervene in your affairs. There are two things that bring down the presence of God:

- Sacrifice on God's altar
- Praise and worship

God will fight those things that oppose your

progress when you bring down His presence by your sacrifice. When you provoke His presence by your sacrifice, He will make your enemies to drink their own blood. He will deliver you even if you were a lawful captive and the prey of the mighty. He is the God of all flesh and nothing is too hard

> *God will fight those things that oppose your progress when you bring down His presence by your sacrifice.*

for Him. Just go ahead and offer a dangerous sacrifice and watch God fight your battle for you.

ISRAEL AND THE PHILISTINES
(I SAM. 7:7-14)

The battle between Israel and the Philistines was so hot that the Israelites told Samuel to pray for them continuously, but instead, Samuel took a suckling lamb and offered it on God's altar. When God saw the sacrifice, He thundered with great thunders against the Philistines and that was the end of the battle.

Friend, have you done all you know how to do and yet no result or solution has come your way? I introduce you to a better and easier way to end this struggle and shame in your life. The answer is sacrifice. Take something of great value and offer it on God's altar today and see if God's presence will not be attracted by that sacrifice of yours to end your sorrows.

Take that car, landed property; close that bank account, if you have to, and bring them to God's altar. Many years ago, somebody in your family spent so much to offer different sacrifices on strange altars which have kept you on the level you are today.

If somebody in the past did that in his ignorance, would you not then be wise enough to change the situation with your present knowledge?

"And the Lord spake unto Moses and Aaron in the land of Egypt, saying, This month shall be unto you the beginning of months: it shall be the first month of the year to you. speak ye unto all the congregation of Israel, saying, In the tenth day of this month they shall take to them every man a lamb, according to the house of their fathers, a lamb for a house: and if the household be too little for the lamb, let him and his neighbour next unto his house take it according to the number of the souls; every man according to his eating shall make your count for the lamb. Your lamb shall

be without blemish, a male of the first year: ye shall take it out from the sheep, or from the goats: and ye shall keep it up until the fourteenth day of the same month: and the whole assembly of the congregation of Israel shall kill it in the evening. And they shall take of the blood, and strike it on the two side posts and on the upper door post of the houses, wherein they shall eat it. And they shall eat the flesh in the night, roast with fire, and unleavened bread; and with bitter herbs they shall eat it. Eat not of it raw, nor sodden at all with water, but roast with fire; his head with his legs, and with the purtenance thereof. And ye shall let nothing of it remain until the morning; and that which remaineth of it until the morning ye shall burn with fire. And thus shall ye eat it; with your loins girded, your shoes on your feet, and your staff in your hand; and ye shall eat it in haste: it is the Lord's Passover. For I will pass through the land of Egypt this night, and will smite all the firstborn in the land of Egypt, both man and beast; and against all the gods of Egypt I will execute judgment: I am the Lord. And the blood shall be to you for a token upon the houses where ye are: and when I see the blood, I will pass over you, and the plaque shall not be upon you to destroy you, when I smite the land of Egypt. And this day shall be unto you for a memorial; and ye shall keep it a feast to the Lord throughout your generations; ye shall keep it a feast by an ordinance forever.

(Exod. 12:1-14)

Before this time, Moses had confronted Pharaoh with nine signs and wonders to demand Israel's release according to God's instruction, but Pharaoh refused. For instance, none of the plaques (water turned into blood, frogs, swarms of flies, darkness, etc) in the land of Egypt brought about the desired effect to make Pharaoh change his mind about letting Israel go. He held the people of God whom God had promised a land flowing with milk and honey.

God had spoken to Abraham in **Gen. 15:13** that his seed shall be strangers in the land that was not theirs for four hundred years and He (God) would deliver them with great substance. But they stayed for four hundred & thirty years. Pharaoh prolonged their stay and suffering.

After the nine plaques had been exhausted, God reserved the weapon of sacrifice for the final onslaught against the enemy. God knew that there was something that would break Pharaoh's power sacrifice. He knew the power of the blood hence He used it to settle that prolonged issue once and for all.

He therefore commanded Moses to tell the children of Israel to sacrifice a lamb or goat and use the blood as a token upon the lintels of their houses. God promised to pass through the land of Egypt that night to execute judgment upon the gods of the Egyptians. He said, *"When I see the blood, I will pass over you."*

God implies here that the only thing that will exempt anybody from His anger was sacrifice. *When I see the sacrifice, I will pass over you.* The blood from the sacrifice on the door lintel of the Israelites was speaking for their freedom. The gods of Egypt spoke against them, but the blood spoke for them. Hallelujah!

The angel of the Lord passed through the land that night and killed all the firstborns of Egypt - both man and beast, but in the houses where there was sacrifice and blood, there was none dead.

By morning, Israel departed from slavery into freedom, from poverty to prosperity just by obeying instruction to sacrifice. The journey of 430 years ended in just one night of obedience.

Your sacrifice will attract God's presence to fight for you.

Friend, God is saying: *'what many prayers and fasting and deliverance have not been able to achieve, sacrifice will achieve.'* Your sacrifice will attract God's presence to fight for you. That night, when God saw the sacrifice from various homes, He came down to deliver his people. The gods of Egypt that had been speaking against God's people, stopped speaking that night when the blood from their sacrifice spoke.

God said, *When I see the blood, I will pass over you. When I see your sacrifice, I will pass you over to the next level of your life. When I see your sacrifice, I will stop the plague in the family. When I see your sacrifice, I will execute judgment on the family spirits that have been against your life. When I see your sacrifice, I will exempt you from the calamity in the family. When I see your sacrifice, I will manifest my power against your enemies. When I see your sacrifice, I will end your sorrow.*

Good friend, do you want God to contend with your Pharaoh? Do you want God to stop the plaque in your life and family? Do you want to move to the place which God has ordained for you? Do you want to be different in your family? Then take a quality sacrifice right now to God's altar and attract His presence for your victory.

Did you know that only those who obeyed God were exempted from the judgment that night?

Only those who sacrificed left Egypt. As many of the Israelites that ignored that simple instruction of sacrificing, were left behind to continue in slavery.

Did you also know that some of the Egyptians, who joined the Israelites to obey God, escaped the judgment and left with them to the Promised Land?

> *"And a mixed multitude went up also with them; and flocks, and herds, even very much cattle."* **(Exod. 12:38)**

The Bible says that those who left Egypt were a mixed multitude. Child of God, I want you to escape right now. If no one else is ready to do it, you must do it for yourself and your seed.

Jacob took them to Egypt in search of solution, but he left them there. Our fathers also took us to the Egypt of family altars and forgot us there, but God has given us the way out sacrifice.

Therefore, you must fight your way out. Your prayers, fasting and deliverance must be backed up with quality sacrifice to end this long-standing issue in your life. The reason is that it was the voice of the sacrifices that empowered the demonic powers that have been speaking against our progress; therefore, it is sacrifice that will still stop their voice from speaking any further. Our sacrifice will disarm all the demonic powers.

ELIJAH AND THE 450 PROPHETS OF BAAL

"And Elijah said unto all the people, Come near unto me. And all the people came near unto him. And he repaired the altar of the Lord that was broken down. And Elijah took twelve stones, according to the number of the tribes of the sons of Jacob, unto whom the word of the Lord came, saying, Israel shall be thy name: and with the stones he built an altar in the name of the Lord: and he made a trench about the altar, as great as would contain two measures of seed. And he put the wood in order, and cut the bullock in pieces, and laid him on the wood, and said, Fill four barrels with water, and pour it on the burnt sacrifice, and on the wood. And he said, Do it the second time. And they did it the second time. And he said, Do it the third time. And they did it the third time. And the water ran round about the altar; and he filled the trench also with water. And it came to pass at the time of the offering of the evening sacrifice, that Elijah the prophet came near, and said, Lord God of

Abraham, Isaac, and of Israel, let it be known this day that Thou art God in Israel, and that I am Thy servant, and that I have done all these things at Thy word. Hear me, O Lord, hear me, that this people may know that Thou art the Lord God, and that Thou hast turned their heart back again. Then the fire of the Lord fell, and consumed the burnt sacrifice, and the wood, and the stones, and the dust, and licked up the water that was in the trench. And when all the people saw it, they fell on their faces: and they said, The Lord, He is the God; the Lord, He is the God." (I Kgs. 18:30-39)

There comes a time in a man's life when he must do something to end the contradictions in his life. That is the issue here. The Israelites have been between two opinions here; they now doubted God's ability and power, hence they chose to serve other gods, an action which God warned them not to indulge in. God knows that if Israel raises another altar and sacrifice on it, they will be led by a strange voice and so He told them that they must not serve any other god beside Him. However, they could not endure some life challenges hence they sought solution from strange gods. So many people today react to issues in life the same way. It did not start with us; it has been in existence.

Elijah, God's prophet, decided to prove that God remains God, no matter the challenges we face. He therefore summoned the prophets of Baal to a contest at Mount Carmel to end the contradiction: the God who answered by fire would be the true and supreme God. The false prophets did not hesitate to take advantage of this to prove to Elijah that Baal was the supreme God, but unfortunately, they were dead wrong. They cried and shouted from morning till the time of the evening sacrifice without any success of bringing fire down from heaven.

In **vs. 30-33,** Elijah repaired the altar of God which had been broken down; he then built a new altar with twelve stones representing the twelve tribes of Israel and he put a new sacrifice on that altar.

In **vs. 36-38,** he called on the God of Abraham, Isaac and Israel and said,

> *"Let it be known this day... Hear me, Oh Lord. Hear me, that this people may know that Thou art the Lord God."*

Vs. 38 reports that the fire of the Lord fell and consumed the burnt sacrifice along with the water and stones.

> *Child of God, the secret of the above*
> *manifestation was not Elijah's prayer but*
> *a new altar and a new sacrifice.*

God simply came down by fire to consume the sacrifice. A new altar and sacrifice attracted His presence, and He thereby ended the controversy. He ended all questions with that answer.

Oftentimes, we call on the God that answers by fire to answer us by fire, but we do not see Him. Why? Is it that He has changed and does not answer by fire as in the days of Elijah anymore? No. The truth is that God, who is the Fire that consumes fire, will only show up when there is sacrifice on the altar. If you need to end the contradiction in your life, then build a new altar and sacrifice on it and you will see the God that answers by fire work in your life.

DAVID AND THE PLAGUE OF DEATH
(2 SAM. 24:15-25)

David had numbered Israel and God's anger had kindled against him. He pleaded for mercy, and God gave him three options of punishment to choose from: 7 years of famine, 3 months of defeat in the hands of his enemies, or 3 days of pestilence. He opted for the last one and in one day alone, 70,000 men died in Israel.

Just through one man's mistake, multitudes died the death they had not planned and did nothing to warrant. Is it not the same thing happening to us today? We suffer the consequences of our fathers' mistakes.

In **vs. 18** however, God sent a prophet to David for him to go to the threshing floor of Araunah and raise an altar and sacrifice there for the plague to stop because in **vs. 17,** David had pleaded with God to spare the people. He prayed and God responded to his prayer by instructing him to raise the altar and sacrifice on it for the plague to be stopped.

David did as the prophet commanded him. Araunah offered to give him everything freely, but he declined, saying, *"Nay, but I will surely buy it of thee at a price: neither will I offer burnt offerings unto the Lord my God of that which doth cost me nothing."*

When David built the altar and offered burnt offering and peace offering on it, God was entreated for the land and the plague stopped. God Almighty, who gave the instruction to angels to kill the people, changed His mind when He saw David's sacrifice.

If God could change His mind on an issue He ordered Himself, who is the devil that God cannot stop what he is illegally inflicting on you and your family?

> *If God could change His mind on an issue He ordered Himself, who is the devil that God cannot stop what he is illegally inflicting on you and your family?*

You have suffered for too long. This plague in your family can stop if only you can do what David did: sacrifice is the answer. This plaque of untimely death, divorce, poverty, sickness, tragedy, etc. will stop when the right sacrifice is offered.

Sometimes, what we give as sacrifice are just convenient offerings that cost us little or nothing, which accounts for why the plague has continued unabated. What do you think would have happened if David had collected the offerings from Araunah and offered what had not cost him anything? Sure, the plague would have continued. Child of God, stop that killing in your family now with your sacrifice.

Hear this: *if you have five cars, and you give one among the oldest ones which you don't even use any more as sacrifice, is that truly a sacrifice that cost you something?*

Now, compare that with the only car of another brother which is relatively of lower quality. Compare the pains and inconveniences and you will understand what true sacrifice is all about. In the same vein, when you give large sums of money out of your abundance, you may not feel any pain, unlike the sister who gives her monthly salary without any hope of where her feeding and other monthly expenditure/dues would come from.

A sacrifice is that which is not convenient for you to release or let go. It is that which pains you to release or causes some inconvenience to your budget or plans for that season. If it does not cost you anything, then it is not a sacrifice.

> *A sacrifice is that which is not convenient for you to release or Let go.*

THE KING OF MOAB AND HIS FIRST SON (2 KGS. 3:1-27)

The Moabites were the descendants of the illegitimate relationship between Lot and his first daughter. In the above chapter, the king of Moab had rebelled against Israel after the death of Ahab. King Jehoram consulted with king Jehoshaphat and the king of Edom to go into war with him against the Moabites so as to compel them to pay tribute to him.

On their way, however, they decided to consult the prophet Elisha to find out God's mind about the intended battle. God gave His approval, as well as details of how they would win the war. He assured them that *the war was but a light thing in His sight;* that He was with them in the battle. God showed His wonders by confusing the Moabites with a reflection of the sun on their water as blood. They thought that the Israelites had smitten themselves and they went for the spoils only to walk into the midst of the ready fully-armed Israelites' army.

Israel smote them and they ran for their lives, being pursued and destroyed, with their cities not spared either.

> *"And when they came to the camp of Israel, the Israelites rose up and smote the Moabites, so that they fled before them: but they went forward smiting the Moabites, even in their country. And they beat down the cities, and on every man his stone, and filled it; and they stopped all the wells of*

> *water, and felled all the good trees: only in Kirharaseth left they the stones thereof; howbeit the slingers went about it, and smote it. And when the king of Moab saw that the battle was too sore for him, he took with him seven hundred men that drew swords, to break through even unto the king of Edom: but they could not. Then he took his eldest son that should have reigned in his stead, and offered him for a burnt offering upon the wall. And there was great indignation against Israel: and they departed from him, and returned to their own land."* (2 Kgs. 3:24-27)

When the king of Moab saw that he was losing the battle, he resorted to his reserved military might the only military hope of seven hundred strong and mighty men of valour, but alas, he lost even them.

At this point therefore, he knew that if he failed to do something, he would loose the residue of both his immediate family and country. As a result, he resorted to the one and last option open to him *sacrifice.* He took his son who would have reigned after him and offered him as a sacrifice for the lives of the remaining people of Moab.

When Israel saw it, they turned from pursuing after him. What happened here? Why did God move Israel to stop at this point? Did He not promise to give them a complete victory over this rebellious king in the first place?

God stopped Israel when He saw the sacrifice of this king. That sacrifice was not to the Lord, so why did God not allow the Israelites to 'finish' the man and the remainder of his people?

The answer is simple: God saw what the king did to rescue the remnant of his people and his land. He saw a type of the sacrifice in His plan for the redemption of mankind. God saw a man who could sacrifice the most precious possession he had for the lives of his people, and His heart was touched to change His mind about destroying them. Child of God, when God saw that action, He changed His mind from what He had earlier told these kings through the prophet Elisha.

Friend, you have to do something to rescue the remaining members of your family. Even if you do not want to sacrifice for your own destiny, why not do it for your children? Do it for your brothers and sisters. Do something to stop the pursuit of the enemy in your life and family. Do something to turn the enemy of your destiny back. Take the most precious, the most important thing you have and drop it on God's altar right now and stop Satan's madness against you.

Take a great sacrifice to end this barrenness, non-achieve-ment, backwardness and poverty in both your life and family. Friend, you can do it *now.* Don't wait any further. Give up that thing which you think is very important and precious to you for your destiny, for what lies ahead of you is far more important and precious than what you have

> *Take the most precious, the most important thing you have and drop it on God's altar right now and stop Satan's madness against you.*

now. Your future is greater than your present. Your tomorrow is far greater than your today; therefore, do something for your tomorrow. Don't consider the inconveniences or the vacuum it will create; God is about to give you more than you can ever dream of. Yes, He is about to take away shame and disgrace from you. He is ready to take you to the next level of your life.

Listen, the devil does not want you to do it, and so he will do everything necessary to stop you. He will not allow you to sacrifice, but you must disobey him this time, for he knows that he will lose the battle once you sacrifice that precious thing that amount, that car, that house or landed property. He knows that your sacrifice will attract the presence of the Spirit of God whose Voice will stop his voice against you. Brother/Sister, the enemy of your destiny knows that his authority over you is empowered by the sacrifices of your fathers, and that yours can totally break that control today.

> *Your future is greater than your present. Your tomorrow is far greater than your today; therefore, do something for your tomorrow.*

Friend, stop him with your sacrifice. Give your seed an opportunity to speak on your behalf. It has worked and is still working for me and countless number of people around the world. There are things my prayers and fasting could not do for me, but which sacrifices on God's altar and seeds at the feet of His prophets have adequately done for me. Because of these, I can confidently say that it works. Do it now and see how it will bring your long-awaited evidence in your life. Sacrifice will make you to testify.

Welcome to your world of ceaseless testimonies! Welcome to your world of undeniable evidence!

PRAYER
POINTS

PRAYER
POINTS

1. In the name of Jesus, I destroy every ancestral altar that is speaking against my destiny

2. Strange altars, hear my voice: Stop speaking against my life!

3. I destroy every covenant operating in my life as a result of the ancient altars in my father's house. Oh you altars! Oh you altars of my fathers, break in Jesus' name.

4. Oh altars of poverty, break by fire in Jesus' name.

5. Oh you altar of divorce, break in Jesus' name.

6. Oh altar against my marriage, scatter by fire in Jesus' name.

7. You altar of witchcraft, stop speaking against my life in Jesus' name.

8. You altar of my village, stop your activities in my life in Jesus' name.

9. Altars from my father's lineage, I break your dominion of my life in Jesus' name.

10. Altars from my mother's lineage, scatter by fire in Jesus' name!

11. You altars of untimely death in my father and mother's lineage, be scattered by Holy Ghost fire in Jesus' name.

12. Oh you altar of barrenness, break by fire!

13. You altar of family sickness, break in Jesus' name.

14. Oh altar of struggle and limitation, break in Jesus' name.

15. I break you altars of shame and disgrace in my family in Jesus' name.

16. I refuse to remain a victim of strange altars in my father's house in Jesus' name.

17. Every spirit on assignment in my life as a result of the altars in my father's house, hear my voice: Your assignment in my life is henceforth terminated in Jesus' name.

18. You altar that has denied me entrance to my next level in life, break in Jesus' name.

19. You wicked altars against my mother's children, scatter in Jesus' name.

20. You strange altars against my father's children, I destroy you in Jesus' name.

21. You altar that speaks against our academic success, scatter by fire in Jesus' name.

22. Every strange altar against my progress in life, break now in Jesus' name.

23. Oh you altars against my prosperity, break by fire in Jesus' name.

24. You wicked altars against my finances, scatter by fire in Jesus' name.

25. In the name of Jesus, I release my destiny from every wicked altar of my ancestors.

26. Every evil altar which I raised by myself in pursuit of solution, and is working against me now, I command you to break now in Jesus' name.

27. Oh Lord, grant me the grace to obey You now in the name of Jesus.

28. By the anointing of the Holy Ghost, I raise a new altar for my life.

29. In the name of Jesus, I present my sacrifice on the new altar

MY SACRIFICE:

- Speak on my behalf
- Speak for my victory
- Speak success into my life
- Speak prosperity
- Speak abundance
- Speak honour
- Speak favour
- Speak great lifting into my life in Jesus' name